Everybody Cooks Rice

Everybody Cooks Rice

by Norah Dooley · illustrations by Peter J. Thornton

M Millbrook Press/Minneapolis

This book is available in two editions:
Library binding by Millbrook Press, a division of Lerner Publishing Group, Inc.
Soft cover by First Avenue Editions, an imprint of Lerner Publishing Group, Inc.
241 First Avenue North
Minneapolis, MN 55401 USA

For reading levels and more information, look up this title at
www.lernerbooks.com.

Dooley, Norah.
  Everybody cooks rice / by Norah Dooley ; illustrations by Peter J. Thornton.
     p.   cm.
  Summary: A child is sent to find a younger brother at dinnertime and is
introduced to a variety of cultures through encountering the many different
ways rice is prepared at the different households visited.
  ISBN 978–0–87614–412–1 (lib. bdg. : alk. paper)
  ISBN 978–0–87614–591–3 (pbk. : alk. paper)
  ISBN 978–0–7613–8293–5 (EB pdf)
  1. Cookery (Rice)—Juvenile literature. [I. Cookery—Rice.] J. Thornton,
Peter, 1956– ill. II. Title. TX809.
R5D66 1991 641.6'318—dc20
                                                        89-23889
Manufactured in the United States
37 - 51289 - 6628 - 6/28/2021

The artist would like to extend special thanks to his international cast of models.

To my families, immediate and extended, and with thanks to JED.
– N.D.

For Barbara
– P.J.T.

My stomach was grumbling. Mom was cooking dinner, and I couldn't wait to sit down and eat. "Carrie, will you go out and find Anthony—dinner is almost ready."

Mom is always asking me to look for Anthony. He's my little brother, and he's such a moocher! If he's not playing ball or hopscotch, he's at a neighbor's house tasting their dinner.

I walked outside and looked up and down the street. I couldn't see
Anthony anywhere, so I went over to Mrs. Darlington's house.
Anthony and I call her Mrs. D. She's our next-door neighbor.

Mr. and Mrs. D. are from Barbados. It was Thursday, so their grandchildren, Sean and Stephanie, were over having their favorite dinner—black-eyed peas and rice. At the front door I could smell fried onions and bacon. It made my mouth water. I ate a small cup of rice and black-eyed peas while Mr. D. told stories about Barbados. People swim there and go fishing—even in December!

Suddenly I remembered I was supposed to be looking for Anthony, so I asked if anyone had seen him. Sean said he'd seen Anthony going into the Diazes' house. I went there next.

When I walked into the kitchen, my friend Fendra Diaz and her little brother, Tito, were cooking dinner because their mom was working late. Tito was telling Fendra that she uses too much spice. Fendra said Tito was checking the pot too often, so the rice and pigeon peas would never cook. Their teenage brother, José, told them to pipe down. He wanted to watch TV.

I looked in the pot to see what was cooking. The rice was bright yellow! Fendra told me that her grandmother in Puerto Rico had taught her how to cook with turmeric. Turmeric makes rice yellow. Tito gave me a taste from the cooking spoon. Boy, was it delicious! Then I asked if anyone had seen Anthony. Fendra said Anthony had been there to taste their dinner but had left to visit Dong. So, I went across the street to Dong's house.

Dong Tran came from Vietnam five years ago with his whole family—aunts, uncles, cousins, and all. Dong's older sister, Tam, answered the door. Mr. and Mrs. Tran work late every day, so everyone else takes turns making dinner. It was Tam's turn to cook. She was busy making the garlicky, fishy sauce, called *nuoc cham*. She let me try it on some rice. It was sweet and salty and sour. It tasted incredible! Later, when Mrs. Tran gets home, she'll make fried rice with peas. When Mr. Tran gets home, everyone will sit down and eat together.

When I asked if anyone had seen my brother, Dong said Anthony had been helping Mrs. Hua and Mei-Li with their groceries. The Huas live on the corner, so I started to walk up the street.

"Carrie, wait up!" someone called. It was my friend Rajit. He was carrying three round metal boxes all clipped together. Something inside smelled delicious, so I asked him what it was. Rajit said his parents were working at their video and gift shop, so he was bringing them leftovers in a tiffin carrier.

There was a big party at the Krishnamurthys' house last weekend, so Rajit's mother cooked a fancy, colorful Indian dish called *biryani*. It's made with peas, cashews, raisins, lots of spices, and a special kind of rice called basmati rice. I had tasted *biryani* at Rajit's house the last time I went out looking for Anthony.

When I told Rajit that I was looking for my brother *again*, he said Anthony and Mei-Li were blowing bubbles out a window of the Huas' house.

The Huas came from China a year ago. Mrs. Hua is just learning how to speak English. We smile at each other a lot.

Mrs. Hua was steaming white rice for her family and the boarder who lives in the back room. She was also making tofu and vegetables in the wok—that's a big pan with a round bottom. Mrs. Hua always makes me sit down and eat something when I come over.

Everyone at the Huas' house uses chopsticks. Mei-Li, who is only three and a half years old, can even pick up a single grain of rice with her chopsticks! Mei-Li laughed at me when I tried using chopsticks and dropped some vegetables. She said Anthony was "bye-bye," so I decided to try our backyard neighbors, the Bleus.

The Bleus are from Haiti. Their cat just had kittens, so Anthony wanders over there a lot. Mrs. Bleu teaches English at the community center. We get to call her Madame Bleu. Madame Bleu speaks three languages—French, English, and Creole.

When I walked in, Madame Bleu was making a creole style Haitian dinner. It had hot peppers, chives, red beans, and you guessed it—rice. Monsieur Bleu works two jobs, so he won't get home till late. Madame Bleu says the pot will stay on the stove, and the rice will get tastier and spicier.

Adeline and Jeanne-Marie Bleu came home for dinner on their break from their after-school jobs at the grocery store. They helped themselves to bowls of rice and beans from the pot, and gave some to me. I thought my mouth was on fire! Jeanne-Marie teased me when I gulped some water.

It was getting late, and I still hadn't found Anthony. Adeline said she had seen him with a kitten in his arms, climbing the fence to our yard. I said thanks and *au revoir*—that means good-bye—and hurried home.

When I walked into the house, Anthony was showing the kitten to our baby sister, Anna. He was explaining to Mom that he was only borrowing the kitten.

Mom was putting dinner on the table. Her grandmother, from northern Italy, taught our grandmother, who taught Mom how to cook *risi e bisi*—rice with green peas. Mom puts butter, grated cheese, and some nutmeg on it. It smelled so good, but my stomach wasn't grumbling anymore. I told Mom that I was too full to eat. Anthony said he wanted to eat his dinner, even though he was full, because he loves rice, and that afternoon he found out that *everybody* cooks rice.

Recipes

Rice

2 cups rice
2½ cups water

1. Bring rice and water to a boil over high heat in a large covered saucepan.
2. Turn heat down to low and let rice simmer for 25 minutes or until all the water is absorbed.
3. Remove from heat and let stand for 10 minutes.
Note: This is a general rice recipe. Cooking instructions vary depending on type of rice used.

Mrs. D's Black-eyed Peas and Rice

2 cups dried black-eyed peas
water
¼ cup vegetable oil
1 medium onion, peeled and chopped
2 slices bacon
1 teaspoon dried thyme
4 cups cooked rice
salt and black pepper to taste

1. Place black-eyed peas in a medium bowl and cover with cold water. Soak overnight.
2. Drain the peas, rinse, then boil in water for 20 minutes or until the black-eyed peas are tender. Drain and rinse the peas.
3. In a Dutch oven, heat the oil over medium heat, and sauté the onion and bacon. Break the bacon into small pieces.
4. Add thyme and stir.
5. Add cooked rice, black-eyed peas, salt, and pepper, stirring thoroughly to mix the ingredients.

The Diazes' Turmeric Rice with Pigeon Peas

1 vegetable or chicken bouillon cube
8 cups water
¼ cup cooking oil
1 green onion, finely chopped
½ teaspoon turmeric
4 cups cooked white rice
1 pound dried pigeon peas, soaked overnight and drained

Use a pot with a tight cover.

1. Dissolve bouillon cube in 1 cup water, then add to the rest of the water. Set aside.
2. In the pot, combine oil, onion, and turmeric, and cook over medium heat until onion is transparent. Turn the heat off right away.
3. Add rice and water with dissolved bouillon cube, and cook for 10 minutes on the highest heat.
4. Lower the heat to medium and add the pigeon peas. Stir a bit and cover.
5. Cook for about 15 minutes or until all the water is gone.

Tam's Nuoc Cham

Fish sauce can be found in any Asian market or the international section of a supermarket.

In a jar combine:
5 tablespoons fish sauce
2 tablespoons lime juice or 4 tablespoons white vinegar
1 peeled and finely grated carrot
3 cloves garlic, peeled and finely chopped or pressed
1 teaspoon crushed red pepper
1 to 1½ cups water
3 tablespoons sugar

1. Cover the jar and shake until the sugar is dissolved.
Note: *Nuoc cham* is used as a dip or a sauce and is usually a part of every Vietnamese meal.

Mrs. Tran's Fried Rice

2 eggs
1 tablespoon butter
1 small onion, peeled and finely chopped
3 tablespoons oil
½ cup green peas
½ cup corn
1 carrot, peeled and grated
1 teaspoon sugar
1 tablespoon fish sauce
2 tablespoons soy sauce
4 cups cold cooked rice

1. Scramble the eggs in butter and set aside.
2. In a wok or large frying pan over medium heat, sauté onion in oil until it's transparent.
3. Add the vegetables and cook, stirring, for three minutes.
4. Add sugar, fish sauce, and soy sauce, and mix well.
5. Add rice and cook for about five minutes, stirring frequently, until all the food is hot.
6. Chop up the scrambled eggs, mix them in, and serve.

Rajit's Biryani

Basmati rice has a special flavor, but any sort of rice will do in a pinch. There should be at least two times as many vegetable and nuts as rice.

2 medium onions, peeled and chopped
2 tablespoons butter
Spices:
    2 cloves garlic, peeled and finely chopped
    2 teaspoons grated fresh ginger
    1 teaspoon ground coriander
    ¼ teaspoon each crushed black pepper, cayenne pepper, ground cloves, ground cinnamon, ground cardamom
    1 teaspoon cumin
Vegetables
    ½ cup carrots, peeled and thinly sliced
    2 fresh tomatoes, peeled, quartered, and diced
    1 cup cauliflower florets
    1 cup green beans
    1 cup green peas
3 cups half-cooked rice (rice that has cooked for 7 to 10 minutes)

2 tablespoons water
½ cup cashews or blanched almonds
½ cup raisins
2 hard-boiled eggs, peeled

1. In a large frying pan over medium heat, sauté onions in 1 tablespoon butter until golden.
2. Add all spices.
3. Add all the vegetables and sauté for 2 or 3 minutes
4. Butter a large casserole dish and add all the ingredients, mixing or layering rice and vegetables.
5. Bake at 300 degrees F for 30–35 minutes.
6. Sauté cashews and raisins in 1 tablespoon butter.
7. Crumble hard-boiled eggs.
8. When biryani is baked, sprinkle with cashews, raisins, and crumbled hard-boiled eggs.

Mrs. Hua's Tofu with Vegetables

1 pound tofu, cut into 1-inch cubes
1 tablespoon soy sauce
1 tablespoon oyster sauce
1 teaspoon sesame oil
1 teaspoon sugar
4 tablespoons vegetable oil
½ teaspoon salt
2 cups green beans, cut into 1-inch lengths
½ cup water chestnuts
½ cup sliced mushrooms

1. Combine tofu, soy sauce, oyster sauce, sesame oil, and sugar. Refrigerate for at least one hour.
2. Heat 2 tablespoons vegetable oil in a wok or high-sided frying pan. Add salt, green beans, water chestnuts, and mushrooms. Cook, stirring constantly, for about two minutes. Pour into a bowl.
3. Add 2 tablespoons vegetable oil to the same wok.
4. Add tofu mixture and stir constantly for about 5 minutes.
5. Return green bean mixture to the wok and mix thoroughly.
6. Serve with cooked rice.

Madame Bleu's Rice and Beans

1 cup red beans
water
½ cup oil
2 slices bacon
2 cloves garlic, peeled and finely chopped
¼ cup chopped parsley
¼ teaspoon cayenne pepper (or more if desired)
1 teaspoon thyme
1 tablespoon chopped chives
4 cups cooked white rice

1. Place red beans in a medium bowl and cover with cold water. Soak overnight.
2. Drain the beans, rinse, then boil in water for 20 minutes or until the beans are tender.
3. Drain the beans and set aside.
4 In a frying pan over medium heat, heat oil and sauté bacon until lightly browned. Break into small pieces.
5. Add garlic, parsley, cayenne pepper, thyme, and chives. Now add the beans and fry gently.
6. Stir bean mixture into the cooked rice. Sprinkle with fresh chives.

Great-Grandmother's Risi e Bisi

2 cubes vegetable or chicken bouillon
4 cups water
1 clove garlic, peeled and finely chopped
1 small onion, peeled and finely chopped
3 tablespoons olive oil
2 cups uncooked rice
2 cups fresh or frozen green peas
½ to 1 cup grated Parmesan cheese
½ teaspoon ground nutmeg

Use a pot with a tight cover.

1. In a bowl, dissolve bouillon cubes in 2 cups of water, then add to the rest of the water. Set aside.
2. Over medium heat, cook garlic and onion in olive oil until the onion is transparent. Don't let the garlic turn brown!
3. Turn off heat right away and pour in rice. Stir in the 4 cups of water and dissolved bouillon and cook on highest heat until mixture boils. Lower heat and do not remove lid. Cook for 25 minutes.
4. If using frozen peas, soak them in warm water. When rice is cooked, add peas, stir in Parmesan cheese, and sprinkle with nutmeg.